The Sioux

D1232209

BIBLIOGRAPHICAL SERIES
*The Newberry Library Center
for the History of the American Indian*

General Editor
Francis Jennings

Assistant Editor
William R. Swagerty

The Center is Supported by Grants from

The National Endowment for the Humanities
The Ford Foundation
The W. Clement and Jessie V. Stone Foundation
The Woods Charitable Fund, Inc.
Mr. Gaylord Donnelley

The Sioux

A Critical Bibliography

HERBERT T. HOOVER

Published for the Newberry Library

Indiana University Press

BLOOMINGTON AND LONDON

Z1210.D3 H65 1979
Hoover, Herbert T.
The Sioux : a critical
bibliography

Copyright © 1979 by Indiana University Press

All rights reserved

No part of this book may be reproduced or utilized in any form or
by any means, electronic or mechanical, including photocopying
and recording, or by any information storage and retrieval system,
without permission in writing from the publisher. The Association
of American University Presses' Resolution on Permissions consti-
tutes the only exception to this prohibition.

Manufactured in the United States of America

Library of Congress Cataloging in Publication Data

Hoover, Herbert T
   The Sioux.

   (Bibliographical series)
   Bibliography: p.
   Includes index.
   1. Dakota Indians—Bibliography. 2. Assiniboin Indians—
Bibliography. I. Title. II. Series.
   Z1210.D3H65   [E99.D1]   016.97'0004'97   79-2167
   ISBN 0-253-34972-9 pbk.   1 2 3 4 5 83 82 81 80 79

CONTENTS

AUTHOR'S PREFACE

In the 1970s, more than 50,000 persons are members of Sioux and related Assiniboine tribes scattered across twenty-seven reservations in five states and three Canadian provinces. Many of those who live on the reserves are poverty-stricken, despite recent efforts by public officials to improve conditions through industrial programs and welfare assistance. They are embroiled in political controversies perpetuated by competition for jobs. They suffer from inadequate housing, deficient health care, inferior education, and other adverse conditions resulting from more than three centuries of contact with non-Indians.

Before French colonials appeared during the 1630s, the Sioux and Assiniboines lived more rewarding lives in the woodlands surrounding the headwaters of the Mississippi River as a loose federation of seven "council fires": Mdewakantons, Wahpekutes, Sissetons, Wahpetons, Tetons, Yanktons, and Yanktonais. They enjoyed an orderly civilization governed by ancient codes and political institutions. They thrived on the abundant food supplies obtained from the luxuriant forests and adjacent prairies, and they were secure under the protection of a league of soldiers' societies. Apparently the only major problem in their late prehistoric existence was a domestic quarrel that sent a small band of Yanktonais into exile on the Manitoba prairies, where their leaders established the Assiniboine tribe.

Otherwise Sioux people lived comfortably in domestic peace, with little concern about affairs beyond their own territorial boundaries. They continued to flourish in the woodlands for nearly a century after French traders and Roman Catholic priests moved out to work among them. With necessities readily available, they had time for religion, philosophy, art, and recreation. Despite an occasional fracas with a neighboring tribe over territorial lines, they still had little cause to worry about security.

In the second quarter of the eighteenth century, however, they experienced a crisis that forced them not only to abandon their woodland territories but also to accept major changes in life-style and culture. Ancient weapons failed to repel an invasion by Ojibwas equipped with European firearms. After a protracted war, the Sioux retreated to the prairies, spread out in new encampments from southeastern Minnesota to the foothills of the Rocky Mountains, and divided their civilization into three components as they adapted to conditions in several physiographic provinces. In the east, *Isantis** (Mdewakantons, Wahpekutes, Sissetons, and Wahpetons) retained the culture of the federation as it had existed before the exodus. Out west, Tetons adopted the customs of neighboring plainsmen. At the

---

*"Isanti" is used because the term "Santee" has been preempted by Mdewakantons and Wahpekutes at Santee, Nebraska, and Flandreau, South Dakota, for use in modern tribal names. Isanti is an older word that was sometimes used to record the presence of Mdewakantons and Wahpekutes, but it seems also to have been employed as a generic term to include all four eastern tribes—Mdewakanton, Wahpekute, Sisseton, and Wahpeton.

center of Sioux country, Yanktons and Yanktonais dis-
played practices and beliefs that resembled those of
both their eastern and western relatives; yet they also
bore traits that were distinctly their own.
While Sioux people adjusted to new conditions,
spokesmen from France, Spain, and later the United
States announced imperial claims to the same region,
which they called Upper Louisiana. For half a century
the intruders did not interfere in the affairs of the
tribes, but during the War of 1812 United States government officials became meddlesome. Federal agents
pressed Isanti chiefs for amity agreements after more
than one hundred eastern Sioux soldiers sided with
British forces at the request of Canadian merchants.
Manuel Lisa founded a subagency in the Missouri
Basin to maintain neutrality among Tetons, Yanktons,
and Yanktonais. War Department leaders laid plans to
bring Sioux people under the control of the United
States.
 After the war these plans were written into treaties.
In 1815, federal officers summoned leaders from several tribes to Portage des Sioux to approve documents
that proclaimed the sovereignty of the United States in
Upper Louisiana. During the 1820s and 1830s, War
Department spokesmen went to Indian country to record the marks of chiefs and headmen from all Sioux
tribes on treaties that forbade further trade between
the Sioux and Canadian merchants, guaranteed peace
between Sioux people and neighboring tribes, and as-
sured the safety of United States citizens, who by then

had begun to settle on the northern prairies in substantial numbers.

Evidently, chiefs and headmen affixed their marks to the treaties with little hesitation, for at the time conditions favored their constituents. Sioux people were still remote from parts of Louisiana where Jacksonian officials instituted a "civilization plan" to prepare native Americans for incorporation into the general society. They enjoyed considerable benefit from trade at outposts run by American merchants along the Mississippi and Missouri rivers and their tributary systems. They were not threatened by United States arms, for War Department officials gradually withdrew military garrisons from Upper Louisiana because they believed bastions on trading posts could provide sufficient defense after all the tribes had accepted treaties.

In these circumstances, the Sioux enjoyed better times than they had known since their migration from the woodlands. Through the second quarter of the nineteenth century they lived in relative isolation, with ample supplies of food and other necessities. By acquiring guns at trading posts and horses from the Great Plains, they built armies that could repel any invading force.

Their last golden era ended abruptly at midcentury, however, for in the 1850s their leaders were summoned for further negotiations to make way for the Anglo-American frontier. In 1851, Tetons, Yanktons, and Yanktonais agreed to the terms of the

Treaty of Fort Laramie, which guaranteed safe passage for overlanders traveling along the southern edge of Sioux country on the Oregon and Mormon trails. That same year, Isanti chiefs and headmen reluctantly signed the treaties of Mendota and Traverse des Sioux, by which they exchanged all their aboriginal land for a small reserve along the upper Minnesota River Valley to accommodate land-hungry farmers. In 1858, Yankton leaders traveled to the national capital and accepted a document that opened the fertile prairies of eastern Dakota to speculators and settlers, concentrated 2,000 Yanktons on a 400,000-acre reservation along the north bank of the Missouri, and called for the immediate implementation of the "civilization plan" on the reserve.

Before most of these treaties were ratified by the United States Senate, Sioux military forces responded with hostilities that were to last for more than three decades and involve all the tribes except the Yanktons. In 1855, Tetons battled General William Harney's unit at Ash Hollow, Nebraska. By this time Tetons were divided into seven distinct groups: Oglalas, Brules, Sans Arc, Two Kettles, Minneconjous, Hunkpapas, and Blackfeet Sioux). Through 1857, Inkpaduta's marauders attacked settlements around Spirit Lake, Iowa, and Jackson, Minnesota. Four years later, Isantis engaged White volunteers in the Minnesota Sioux War. Later in the 1860s, Sitting Bull attacked forts on the upper Missouri and Red Cloud fought to prevent the construction of the Bozeman Trail. In the mid-1870s, more than 20,000 Sioux rallied around Sitting Bull to challenge the United States Army in the Great Sioux War, and subsequently Indian nationalists led resistance movements that did not end until the assassination of Sitting Bull and the massacre at Wounded Knee.

Indian forces won dramatic victories, highlighted by the annihilation of George Custer's cavalry, but in the end their resistance was futile. Gradually the United States Army gained ascendancy. Federal commissioners presented still more treaties and agreements. Miners, cattlemen, farmers, and other groups filed in, and by the early years of the twentieth century Sioux people were confined to small farms on sixteen reservations in five states, where they were subjected to preparation for United States citizenship by federal agents, missionaries, and teachers who were dedicated to their acculturation.

Since 1930, reservation conditions have improved somewhat. Superintendents, missionaries, and teachers have become more flexible. Cultural imperialism has been tempered by the influence of such officials as John Collier. Congress has supplied funds for many programs: direct relief and revolving credit in the 1930s and 1940s; rehabilitation projects and unemployment assistance during the 1950s; poverty programs through the 1960s; claims payments, educational supports, housing programs, welfare assistance, and other programs into the 1970s. But most Americans now recognize that these improvements have not compensated for the loss of land and cultural change the Sioux experienced during their first three hundred years of contact with non-Indians, or for the shabby conditions many of them have endured on reservations in recent years. Canadian Sioux have had similar experiences over the past century. Their societies were established by Isanti and Teton refugees from the Minnesota and Great Sioux wars who remained north of the forty-ninth parallel for fear of reprisals. As conditions demanded, they scattered in small groups on nine tiny reserves that Canadian officials gave them, ostensibly as payment for Isanti support during the War of 1812. Until World War II, they neither received help nor suffered interference from the dominion, but since the war they have been subjected to acculturationist schemes as rigorous as those practiced in the United States.

Assiniboines emerged from approximately three centuries of seminomadic isolation to settle on two reservations in Montana and one in southwestern Canada during the late 1800s. Here they have retained separate identity under the Indian policies of the United States and Canada.

Perhaps the most remarkable feature in the history of the Sioux and Assiniboine people has been their ability to resist compelling forces that have worked to replace their own habits, beliefs, and legacies with those of Anglo-Americans. Despite acculturationist efforts by public officials, missionaries, teachers, and

non-Indian neighbors, factions in all the tribes have
preserved native American languages, devotional
practices, philosophies, and folklore.

Readers should be aware that literature about the
Sioux and Assiniboines fails to touch upon important
dimensions of their past experience. The general history of all identifiable groups of native Americans
exists as three distinct components: the history of
policies devised by non-Indian reformers and political
leaders and enforced by federal officials; the histories
of the internal affairs of all the tribes; and the history
of contact between Indian and non-Indian groups
from the arrival of the first European immigrants to
the present. Published materials on the Sioux and Assiniboines include very little information about United
States and Canadian policies devised expressly for
them, and they deal with intratribal affairs only in cultural studies and reminiscences. Accordingly, the
greatest body of information pertains to relationships
between these Indian groups and the non-Indians with
whom they have been compelled to deal.

No single volume surveys the entire history of contact between the Sioux and Assiniboine tribes and
non-Indians or describes all the traditions that tribal
members have preserved in the face of intense cultural
imperialism. Information about these subjects is scattered in some five thousand books and articles. The
two hundred and thirteen sources described on the fol-
lowing pages will probably satisfy the interests of most
readers.

RECOMMENDED WORKS

For the Beginner

[3] Allen, Clifford, et al. *History of the Flandreau Santee Sioux Tribe.*

[31] Cash, Joseph H. *The Sioux People (Rosebud).*

[40] Deloria, Ella C. *Speaking of Indians.*

[86] Howard, James Henri. *The Dakota or Sioux Indians.*

[162] Robinson, Doane. *A History of the Dakota or Sioux Indians.*

For a Basic Library Collection

[15] Black Elk. *Black Elk Speaks.*

[26] Buechel, Eugene, S.J. *A Dictionary of the Teton Dakota Sioux Language.*

[32] Cash, Joseph H., and Herbert T. Hoover, eds. *To Be An Indian.*

BIBLIOGRAPHICAL ESSAY

General Histories

The Tribes

Two substantial books survey the histories of more than one tribe in the Sioux federation: Doane Robinson's *History of the Dakota or Sioux Indians* [162], which has been printed several times since its initial publication in 1904, and Roy W. Meyer's *History of the Santee Sioux* [128], a more recent study. Robinson's journalistic volume deals with important experiences of all Sioux tribes from their prehistory to the end of the nineteenth century. Meyer's more scholarly work describes the contact history of the Isantis from their initial encounters with non-Indians to the 1960s.

Other tribal studies deal with the plight of individual tribes during critical periods since the outset of the nineteenth century. "Mdewakanton Band of Sioux Indians" [83], by Harold Hickerson, and "Ethnohistorical Report on the Yankton Sioux" [210], by Alan R. Woolworth—both unpolished reports prepared for presentation before the Indian Claims Commission— supply information about the location and condition of the Isantis and Yanktons before hostilities broke out in the 1850s. *Spotted Tail's Folk* [94], by George E. Hyde, surveys the history of the Brules down to the 1890s. *Red Cloud's Folk* [92] and *A Sioux Chronicle* [93], also by Hyde, and *Red Cloud and the Sioux Problem* [142], by

James C. Olson, contain information about the history of the Oglalas from their earliest contacts with non-Indians to the massacre at Wounded Knee in 1890. *Dakota Twilight* [131], by Edward A. Milligan, is an amateurish book about conditions on Standing Rock Reservation in the last quarter of the nineteenth century that has value because it includes Indian viewpoints recorded by its author during the 1930s.

History of the Sisseton-Wahpeton Sioux Tribe [17], prepared by Elijah Blackthunder with participation by several other tribal members, deals with important developments on the Sisseton Reservation during the same period. It has special value for the information it contains about a constitutional republic headed by Chief Gabriel Renville in those years of tribal readjustment and for the legends it preserves in a supplement. Clifford Allen's *History of the Flandreau Santee Sioux Tribe* [3], also published with active participation by tribal members, is a more scholarly survey of the fascinating history of the Flandreau tribe from its establishment by Isanti homesteaders late in the 1860s until the early 1970s.

The Sioux People (Rosebud) [31], by Joseph H. Cash, is a brief but reliable history of the Brules of Rosebud that emphasizes the effect of federal policies upon them in the twentieth century. *The Forgotten Sioux* [172], by Ernest Lester Schusky, deals with the experiences of the Lower Brules on their reservation along the west bank of the Missouri River since the outset of the twentieth century and calls attention to the ability of traditionalists among them to accept change without surrendering cultural traditions and practices. Together these volumes on tribal experiences touch upon most major developments in the history of contact between the Sioux and non-Indians in the United States. In addition, there are three pictorial publications that illustrate life on two large Sioux reservations between the 1880s and the 1920s. John Alvin Anderson's *The Sioux of the Rosebud* [7] and Paul Dyck's *Brule: The Sioux People of Rosebud* [52] both contain reproductions of photographs taken by Anderson on Rosebud Reservation in that period. Amos Bad Heart Bull's *Pictographic History of the Oglala Sioux* [11] presents photographs and illustrations prepared by its author at Pine Ridge.

Special Monographs

Half a dozen special studies delve into the effects of particular events and developments caused by Sioux-White contact during the past 125 years. Remi A. Nadeau's scholarly *Fort Laramie and the Sioux Indians* [136] appraises the effects of non-Indian migration along the Oregon Trail upon the Brules and Oglalas during the second half of the nineteenth century. Gordon Macgregor's *Warriors without Weapons* [122] evaluates the influence of government policies on Indian society around Pine Ridge before World War II and points out the importance of financial assistance to the advancement of individuals there. Robert H.

Ruby's *The Oglala Sioux* [165] gives an Indian Bureau official's assessment of the history of federal policy on the same reservation, plus arguments in favor of the "termination" program in progress at the time of its publication. Eileen Maynard and Gayla Twiss, *That These People May Live* [127], a Public Health Service report, outlines conditions around Pine Ridge in recent years.

Ernest Lester Schusky's *Politics and Planning in a Dakota Indian Community* [171] is a unique report on the use of federal funds paid as compensation for the loss of "taking areas" from reservations along the Missouri River during the construction of main stem dams in the 1950s. Although it deals only with the socioeconomic rehabilitation program established on Lower Brule Reservation by the use of special allocations, it illustrates planning and social reconstruction techniques that were used on most Sioux reservations in the period after World War II.

Harry H. Anderson's "Fur Traders as Fathers" [6] is the only serious publication available on the important roles played by mixed-bloods in modern Sioux history. It traces the experiences of the progeny of Sioux mothers and White fathers from their origins on the fur-trading frontier to their rise to power in Rosebud tribal affairs late in the 1880s.

Autobiographies and Biographies

Sitting Bull

Closely related to tribal studies and special monographs are publications about the lives of individuals who have guided Sioux societies. No person has received more attention in literature about the Sioux than Sitting Bull—the military leader turned medicine man who devoted his life to Sioux nationalism from his rise to the head of a warrior society during the 1850s to his tragic death on Standing Rock Reservation in December 1890. The Hunkpapa leader wrote the first life story himself, in pictographic reminiscences of heroic deeds that have been published as *Three Pictographic Autobiographies of Sitting Bull*, by Matthew William Stirling [182]. Since his death, numerous writers have prepared book-length biographies. In 1891 Willis Fletcher Johnson published *The Red Record of the Sioux* [98], in which he vented anti-Indian bias that is offensive to modern readers, but his book is valuable because it preserves impressions about Sitting Bull's public career that would otherwise have been lost. Next, Stanley Vestal wrote his dramatic *Sitting Bull* [196] from extensive documentary research and many personal interviews. Despite his use of literary license in his interpretations, Vestal created the best general account of this Hunkpapa's career. Subsequently, others wrote books of lesser quality that are worth reading largely because of the additional information they contain:

Doris Shannon Garst's *Sitting Bull* [68], Richard O'Connor's *Sitting Bull* [139], and Dorothy M. Johnson's *Warrior for a Lost Nation* [97].

Publications of narrower scope provide more detailed descriptions of significant events and dramatic episodes in the Hunkpapa leader's life. "Sitting Bull's Own Narrative of the Custer Fight" [166], edited by Walter N. Sage, is an account of the Battle of the Little Big Horn allegedly recorded by Major L. E. F. Crozier during Sitting Bull's Canadian exile. "Sitting Bull: Indian without a Country" [147], by Gary Pennanen, deals with international tensions that resulted from his appearance in Canada after the Custer fight. *Sitting Bull: The Years in Canada* [120], by John Walter Grant MacEwan, describes his experiences north of the border. *The Surrender of Sitting Bull* [4], by Edwin H. Allison, and *Tales from Buffalo Land* [27], by Usher Lloyd Burdick, tell why Sitting Bull gave himself up to United States authorities at Fort Buford in 1881.

No one has prepared a detailed description of his experiences during his confinement at Fort Randall or of his contest with Agent James McLaughlin for control of Standing Rock society during the 1880s, but several authors have described his violent death. McLaughlin wrote his perceptions of conditions that led to the assassination, which are available in *My Friend the Indian* [125]. Edmond Gustav Fechet, the officer in command at the scene where Sitting Bull was shot, recorded the sequence of events immediately preceding the attack in "The Capture of Sitting Bull" [61].

Usher Lloyd Burdick tried to synthesize information about the assassination in *The Last Days of Sitting Bull* [28].

Crazy Horse

The legacy of resistance to White intrusion handed down by Crazy Horse has also attracted writers. Mari Sandoz's *Crazy Horse* [167] is the most substantial book about his life and times, even though it is as much a historial novel as a biography. Doris Shannon Garst's *Crazy Horse* [69] is a similar work, based upon reputable sources, that blends facts with fiction in a narrative intended to attract school-age readers. Stephen E. Ambrose's *Crazy Horse and Custer* [5] presents parallel accounts of the activities of the Sioux leader and his principal adversary in the years before the Battle of the Little Big Horn, and Alvin M. Josephy's *The Patriot Chiefs* [101] includes a chapter-length biography that identifies the major roles Crazy Horse played during his brief and stormy career.

Other sources deal with his last days. In "Crazy Horse's Story of the Custer Battle" [46], Charles Diehl has printed an account of the Battle of the Little Big Horn that Crazy Horse shared with a news correspondent shortly before his violent death. In Earl Alonzo Brininstool's *Crazy Horse* [20], and Robert A. Clark's *The Killing of Chief Crazy Horse* [34], two other editors have presented the "inside story" of how the war chief was slain at Fort Robinson in 1877, as told by Dr. V. T.

McGillycuddy, General Jesse Lee, Chief He Dog, and
others.

Red Cloud

Red Cloud has been slighted. One possible expla-
nation is that he was not as flamboyant as either Sitting
Bull or Crazy Horse. Another is that he decided, after
initial battles against White intruders, to resist
acculturation more through negotiation than through
overt resistance and thereby earned a reputation for
appeasement. In any event, the only studies of his life
prepared by serious writers are those included in
George E. Hyde's *Red Cloud's Folk* [92] and *A Sioux
Chronicle* [93] and in James C. Olson's *Red Cloud and the
Sioux Problem* [142].

Others

The failure of biographers to write about other
influential nineteenth-century political leaders, such as
Spotted Tail at Rosebud and Struck-by-the-Ree on
Yankton Reservation, has left a vacuum in popular literature about tribal affairs on most of the reserves. But
scattered bits of information about less famous persons
can be gleaned from various sources. "The Successive
Chiefs Named Wabasha" [207], by Charles C. Willson,
deals with an important Isanti dynasty. "Reminiscences
of Little Crow" [37], by Asa W. Daniels, touches upon

the life of the man who reluctantly accepted leadership in the Minnesota Sioux War. *Warpath* [197], by Stanley Vestal, and *The Warrior Who Killed Custer* [87], by James Henri Howard, record the personal recollections of White Bull, nephew of Sitting Bull, who participated in the Battle of the Little Big Horn. "Joseph Renville of Lac Qui Parle" [1], by Gertrude W. Ackermann, is about a trader with enormous influence along the upper Minnesota River Valley in the second quarter of the nineteenth century who cooperated with missionaries in preparing the first dictionary and reader published in a Sioux dialect.

Hundreds of Sioux served as scouts for the United States Army during the second half of the nineteenth century. Their motives and roles have never been systematically explored, but two books provide a glimpse of the wealth of information available about them. Ben Innis's *Bloody Knife* [95] tells the story of Custer's favorite scout. It is offensive for its anti-Indian bias, but it explains why a Hunkpapa-Assiniboine mixed-blood defected from the camps of Sitting Bull and Gall to side with the enemy during the wars of the 1860s and 1870s. Henry Hastings Sibley's *Iron Face* [173] relates a fascinating tale about the activities in the Minnesota conflict of a man of Mdewakanton and Scottish descent.

Reminiscences give some insight into the lives of distinguished Sioux humanists who have shared the legacies of their Indian forebears with Indians and non-Indians alike. *Indian Boyhood* [53] and *From the*

Deep Woods to Civilization [57] describe the early experiences of Charles Alexander Eastman, a Dartmouth-educated member of the Flandreau tribe who served as physician on Pine Ridge Reservation during the Wounded Knee massacre, gave important service to the refinement of tribal rolls during the allotment of land, then devoted his life to writing. *My Indian Boyhood* [178] is the autobiography of Luther Standing Bear, a Teton who wrote expressly to explain the habits and inclinations of Indians to White people. *Oscar Howe: The Story of an American Indian* [132], prepared from personal interviews by John Ronald Milton, is the only life story available on this eminent Sioux artist.

Five other sources supply brief sketches of the lives of many individuals who have affected contact history. Indian author Virginia Driving Hawk Sneve's *They Led the Nation* [174] is composed of one- or two-page essays on twenty Sioux leaders. Thomas L. McKenney and James Hall's *History of the Indian Tribes of North America* [124] mentions the elder Little Crow, Wabasha II, and two Yanktons who were prominent during the first half of the nineteenth century. Thomas Hughes's *Indian Chiefs of Southern Minnesota* [90] deals mainly with Isanti leaders. The United States Bureau of Indian Affairs' *Famous Indians* [190] gives summary accounts of the careers of Sitting Bull, Crazy Horse, and Red Cloud. Stephen Return Riggs's "Dakota Portraits" [160] recognizes persons of lower station he knew during the nineteenth century, such as the Indian wife of Joseph Renville.

Battles and Wars

General Accounts

Tribal studies and biographies deal with some aspects of military affairs, but readers must turn to other publications for detailed information about the fights that raged from the battle of Ash Hollow in 1855 to the massacre at Wounded Knee in 1890. In a revisionist article titled "The Winning of the West" [205], Richard White has provided background for the prolonged struggle. He has argued that the western Sioux, after leaving the woodlands, had engaged in a series of successful aggressive wars against their Indian neighbors "largely for the potential economic and social benefits to be derived from furs, slaves, better hunting grounds, and horses." By the middle of the nineteenth century, the Tetons had defeated all Indian adversaries on the northern Great Plains and were only deprived of complete control of the region by the non-Indians who appeared in ever-increasing numbers. Although White oversimplified complex developments he nevertheless has supplied the most realistic description available, and has created a fairly accurate picture of the strength of the Indian forces that challenged non-Indian intruders on the northern Plains during the 1850s.

Several authors have surveyed the causes, progress, and effects of more than one confrontation in the struggle that followed. With both the anti-Indian bias and the empathy characteristic of White contemporaries, Alexander Berghold wrote *The Indians' Revenge* [14] on the Minnesota Sioux War, the Great Sioux War, and the Wounded Knee massacre. Influenced by the mood of the 1960s, Dee A. Brown maligned the intentions of non-Indians during the same conflicts in his book *Bury My Heart at Wounded Knee* [21], as did Alban Williamson Hoopes in *The Road to the Little Big Horn —and Beyond* [84]. Jesse Wendell Vaughn achieved greater objectivity with *Indian Fight* [195], in which he exposed new evidence on the Sioux wars between 1864 and 1879 uncovered by his extensive research and personal observation at the battlegrounds. Newsman Ralph K. Andrist also wrote with little prejudice as he prepared *The Long Death* [8], a readable description of the causes and effects of the Minnesota Sioux War, the Battle of the Little Big Horn, and the massacre at Wounded Knee. And Robert M. Utley prepared a balanced, scholarly account of events from the Little Big Horn to Wounded Knee in *Frontier Regulars* [194] which is excellent for understanding the problems facing the United States Army as well as the Indians of the Plains during the late nineteenth century.

Ash Hollow and Spirit Lake

Books and articles of varying quality are available on each of the several skirmishes and wars. An essay on the initial confrontation, "Reminiscences of the Indian Fight at Ash Hollow, 1855" [50], by Richard C. Drum,

describes General Harney's expedition against Teton
perpetrators of an earlier incident near Fort Laramie.
The book *History of the Spirit Lake Massacre* [112] is an
emotional diatribe on Inkpaduta's escapades given to
its author, Lorenzo Porter Lee, by Abigail Gardner
after she returned from several months of captivity.
"The Ink-pa-du-ta Massacre of 1857" [64], by Charles
Eugene Flandreau, contains the views of a prominent
figure in contemporary Minnesota affairs. "Causes and
Results of the Inkpaduta Massacre" [89], published
later by Thomas Hughes, summarizes the contents of
previous reports left by contemporaries, and *The Spirit
Lake Massacre* [184], by Thomas Teakle, is a more
scholarly treatise on the causes and effects of Inkpaduta's
attacks.

Minnesota Sioux War, 1862–65

More contemporaries wrote about the general war
between Isantis and their non-Indian neighbors that
began several years later. All betrayed intense prejudice as they wrote, but their works are valuable both as
descriptions of principal events and as records of the
racism that accompanied the war. *History of the Sioux
War and Massacres* [81], by an attorney, Isaac V. D.
Heard, is of special interest because it deals with the
treatment of Indians as criminals after the war ended.
Dakota War Whoop [119], by a schoolteacher, Harriet E.
Bishop McConkey, preserves the views of White

participants about the causes, battles, hangings, and postwar punitive expeditions. *Indian Outbreaks* [24], written forty years after the war by a Minnesota supreme court justice, Daniel Buck, traces the course of events from the Spirit Lake Massacre to the end of the Minnesota War, giving special attention to stories of the cruel treatment of non-Indians by Indian soldiers. "Reminiscences of the Little Crow Uprising" [38], by Asa W. Daniels, contains the impressions of a sensitive physician who worked among the Isantis for years before the outbreak began.

Two books published several decades after the war's end purported to deal with the conflict without bias. Because they omitted Indians' viewpoints, neither presented balanced information, but both were important. *Minnesota in the Civil and Indian Wars* [134], prepared by a special commission, revealed statistics on non-Indian military operations as well as eyewitness accounts of the battles. *Recollections of the Sioux Massacre* [199], by Oscar Garrett Wall, condensed contemporary accounts into a general history with success sufficient to earn praise from Mark Twain for both its contents and its "literary excellence."

Recent publications prepared in observance of the centennial of the Isanti conflict are more palatable to readers who wish to learn about it without exposure to the emotions that caused it. Louis Harry Roddis's *The Indian Wars of Minnesota* [163] is a substantial book that traces hostilities from the Spirit Lake Massacre to the postwar punitive expeditions of generals Sibley and

Sully. Charles M. Oehler's *The Great Sioux Uprising* [140] is an interesting journalistic narrative based upon published documents and secondary sources. Robert Huhn Jones's *The Civil War in the Northwest* [100] gives a reliable description of the uprising, and Paul Sanford's *Sioux Arrows and Bullets* [170] is an account of military campaigns against Little Crow based largely upon manuscripts and public documents.

Unfortunately, there are only two publications that reflect the views of Indians. Kenneth A. Carley's "As Red Men Viewed It: Three Indian Accounts of the Uprising" [30] contains information recorded by newsmen late in the nineteenth century, and Gabriel Renville's "A Sioux Narrative of the Outbreak in 1862, and of Sibley's Expedition in 1863" [156] relates the impressions of the mixed-blood who later won Sibley's support for the establishment of his Sisseton republic.

Sibley's postwar expedition out of Minnesota in pursuit of Indian participants is also described in Nathaniel West's *The Ancestry, Life, and Times of Hon. Henry Hastings Sibley, LL. D.* [204]—a book based upon extensive research that was prepared to lavish praise upon the popular general. Accounts of a similar expedition from Sioux City up the Missouri River Valley in pursuit of Indian refugees are available in David L. Kingsbury's "Sully's Expedition against the Sioux in 1864" [105] and in Louis Pfaller's "Sully's Expedition of 1864: Featuring the Killdeer Mountain and Badlands Battles" [149]. Information about the reception given Sioux refugees who escaped capture and reached

Canada is contained in Alvin C. Gluek's "The Sioux Uprising: A Problem in International Relations" [72].

The Great Sioux War of 1876

No single work has appeared to describe Red Cloud's War of the late 1860s, which culminated in the Fetterman massacre, but the war of the mid-1870s has inspired almost countless publications. For half a century or more, most of the literature appeared in the form of editorial polemics and periodical attacks that would have little value to a general reader, but in recent years numerous good books have appeared on the Great Sioux War.

Donald D. Jackson's scholarly monograph *Custer's Gold* [96] traces the course of a reconnaissance expedition into the Black Hills that stimulated the gold rush that precipitated the war. Mari Sandoz's *The Battle of the Little Bighorn* [169] explores reasons behind the expedition against Sitting Bull's army on the Little Big Horn in a semifictional but instructive narrative, and Edgar Irving Stewart's *Custer's Luck* [181] traces the movement of the Seventh Cavalry in a more scholarly account. John S. Gray's *Centennial Campaign* [75] covers the same subjects in a brief survey written for military buffs, and John Frederick Finerty's *War-Path and Bivouac* [62] contains accounts of both the fight on the Little Big Horn and the postwar expedition that drove Sitting Bull into Canada.

As Sitting Bull led more than a thousand followers

across the international border to join Isantis in exile, most of the western Sioux people surrendered their arms and ponies and settled near agencies, where federal officials and missionaries laid plans to enforce the government's "civilization plan." By the time Sitting Bull returned, traditionalists at each agency had established techniques of resistance, and after he came back they worked more vigorously to foil the plan of acculturation to which they were subjected. Their determination was further intensified as federal officials worked through the 1880s to purchase land in the Black Hills region, and it reached a high point of development as they participated in a devotional liturgy called the Ghost Dance. Because Sitting Bull was still the principal symbol of resistance to acculturation, federal officials sought to extinguish the religious practice with his arrest. When the Hunkpapa leader's supporters intervened, he was killed, and a short time later many others died at Wounded Knee on Pine Ridge Reservation.

On the massacre at Wounded Knee, William Fitch Kelley's *Pine Ridge, 1890* [103] presents the observations of a non-Indian who lived nearby. James McGregor's *The Wounded Knee Massacre* [123] is a compilation of stories about the event collected among Sioux people, and Will Spindler's *Tragedy Strikes at Wounded Knee* [176] contains Indian views gathered by an employee of the Indian Service. These publications are valuable, but they should be read only after the reader has studied the contents of Robert Utley's *The*

Last Days of the Sioux Nation [193], the most important work about the causes and meaning of the episode.

Wounded Knee 1973

Writings on the second confrontation at Wounded Knee are largely emotional diatribes in newspaper and periodical articles that express intense bias against either Indians or Whites. But two book-length publications provide insight into the background for the recent takeover. Edward A. Milligan's *Wounded Knee 1973* [130] identifies United States Indian policy as the cause of the anguish that found expression at Wounded Knee in 1973. Bill Zimmerman's *Airlift to Wounded Knee* [213] is composed of some chapters on historical background interspersed with others about mercy flights to Pine Ridge Reserve. Both are worth reading, but readers should review their contents with the knowledge that no reliable book, based upon scholarly research, has yet appeared on this complicated affair.

The Sioux and the United States Government

Major treaties and agreements between the United States government and the Sioux tribes are reproduced in Charles J. Kappler's *Indian Treaties 1778–1883* [102], the standard reference work on Indian treaties, and in George E. Fay's *Treaties and Land Cessions* [60], which contains only treaties and land cession agreements of

the Sioux for the period 1805–1906. Information
about the treaties and the two agreements that established them bringing the reduction of the Great Sioux
Reservation west of the Missouri River, is also available
in *The Sioux Nation and the United States* [137], a publication by the National Indian Defense Association.

Two Indian authors have written polemics on the
failure of federal officials to honor the terms of Indian
treaties and on the policies they have enforced on reservations established by the treaties and agreements. In
Behind the Trail of Broken Treaties [42], Vine Deloria, Jr.
has castigated public officials for their duplicity and has
recommended independent actions by reservation residents as a remedy. In *Custer Died for Your Sins* [41], the
same author has assailed both the motives and the actions of public officials in their relationships with Sioux
people. In *The Tortured Americans* [29], a former
Rosebud tribal chairman, Robert Burnette, has supported Deloria's position and extended the attack
against the whole of non-Indian society. With a similar
purpose, Roxanne Dunbar Ortiz has edited *The Great
Sioux Nation* [143]. Basing her work upon recent tes-
timony by Indian people during federal hearings about
the history of Sioux-government relations, she calls
attention to the "struggle" of Sioux people for
"sovereignty."

Other authors have written articles and books
about narrower aspects of the history of Sioux-federal
relations. In "Federal Indian Policy and the Dakota
Indians: 1800–1840" [146], Howard W. Paulson pro-

vides a useful sketch for the period of initial contact. In "Autobiography of Maj. Lawrence Taliaferro" [183], by the agent who served at Fort Snelling in the period 1819–40, there is interpretation of early federal policies by an official who worked to enforce them. In *Forts of the Upper Missouri* [10], by Robert G. Athearn, there is an excellent description of the movement of the United States Army into Sioux country during the nineteenth century; and, in Francis Paul Prucha's *American Indian Policy in Crisis* [155], one finds an account of the Tetons' relationships with federal officials as they negotiated the reduction of Indian land in the Black Hills region during the 1870s and 1880s. In "The Indian Ring in Dakota Territory" [150], by George H. Phillips, there are tales of fraud among Indian agents, highlighted by the corrupt dealings of Walter Burleigh on the Yankton Reservation and by the irregular practices of V. T. McGillycuddy at Pine Ridge. *Official Relations between the United States and the Sioux Indians* [186], by Lucy Elizabeth Textor, presents an excellent summary of relationships between Sioux tribes and the United States government down to the end of the nineteenth century.

Three books give the views of United States Indian agents about their relationships with Sioux people: Julia Blanchard McGillycuddy's *McGillycuddy, Agent* [121], James McLaughlin's *My Friend the Indian* [125], and DeWitt Clinton Poole's *Among the Sioux or Dakota* [153]. All are apologies for the Indian Service, but they reveal the problems confronted by agents who served on Sioux reservations late in the nineteenth century.

On twentieth-century affairs, Sister Mary Antonio Johnston's *Federal Relations with the Great Sioux Indians of South Dakota* [99] shows how the loss of land affected Sioux societies before World War II, and Joseph H. Cash and Herbert T. Hoover's *To Be an Indian* [32] describes the effects of federal Indian policy upon Sioux people from the late nineteenth-century to the 1970s, in the words of Indians themselves.

Only two publications are available on Sioux relations with the Indian Claims Commission—the special agency created by Congress in 1946 to process suits against the government for the unconscionable treatment of Indians in the past. The agency's own "Commission Findings on the Sioux Indians" [192] is a compilation of information about various Sioux dockets, and Herbert T. Hoover's "Yankton Sioux Tribal Claims against the United States" [85] is a history of claims presented before the commission by one of the tribes.

Several reports describe the experiences of Sioux people with formal education sponsored by federal, state, and local governments. Charles R. Kutzlieb's "Educating the Sioux" [107] deals with the methods, purposes, and politics of Indian education during the post-Civil War era. John Artichoker and Neil M. Palmer, *The Sioux Indian Goes to College* [9], discusses problems that have hampered Sioux students in higher educational institutions in recent years. John Francis Bryde's *The Sioux Indian Student* [22] appraises the influence of cultural differences upon the achievements and attitudes of Sioux students. Arthur M.

Harkins's *Public Education of the Prairie Island Sioux* [79] and Murray Lionel Wax's *Formal Education in an American Indian Community* [203] address the personal problems of Indian children who have attended both integrated schools and segregated reservation schools.

Observations and Influences of Non-Indian Groups

Explorers and Traders

Because explorers and traders were first among non-Indian groups to establish close contact with Sioux people on the prairies and the Great Plains during the first half of the nineteenth century, their diaries and reports contain the most reliable information about the location, composition, and condition of each tribe during that period. First among these observers to take copious notes were Meriwether Lewis and William Clark, whose observations are available in several editions, the best of which is Reuben Gold Thwaites's *Original Journals of the Lewis and Clark Expedition* [189]. Then came Zebulon Montgomery Pike, whose records on the Sioux have been published in Elliott Coues's *Expeditions* [35]. After Pike came trader-agent Manuel Lisa, whose impressions appear in Richard Edward Oglesby's excellent *Manuel Lisa and the Opening of the Missouri Fur Trade* [141].

Two decades later, George Catlin rode the steamboat *Yellowstone* on its initial voyage up the Missouri and took notes as he preserved his observations on canvas. His writings have been published in his *Letters and Notes*

[33]. Several years after Catlin's visit, Joseph Nicollet traversed Upper Louisiana on several expeditions and kept diaries that deal with the locations, populations, languages, and mores of several Sioux tribes. These have been translated and published by Edmund C. and Martha Coleman Bray in *Joseph N. Nicollet on the Plains and Prairies* [19]. Finally, Edwin Thompson Denig, who married an Assiniboine and traded among tribes along the Missouri for twenty-five years, recorded observations on Indian politics, culture, and economy. His records have appeared in his *Five Indian Tribes of the Upper Missouri* [43].

Catholic Missionaries

Close behind traders and explorers came missionaries, the first of whom were regular clergymen of the Roman Catholic church. Jesuits of the seventeenth century kept detailed records, which are available in *The Jesuit Relations* [188], a seventy-three volume set, edited by Reuben Gold Thwaites, that contains bits of information about Sioux people that are accessible through an index. Readers who cannot afford the time required to find information in this fashion are directed to the reminiscences of the Franciscan Louis Hennepin, who was "captured" by Isantis along the Mississippi in 1680 and who later wrote *A New Discovery* [82]. Although Hennepin did not understand the culture he encountered, he prepared the first narrative about its principal dimensions——political organization, religious practices, philosophical inclinations, economy, and life-style.

No other priest bothered to write about his experiences before the Sioux were driven from the woodlands during the second quarter of the eighteenth century, and after that Catholic evangelists avoided Sioux country until 1839, when Pierre Jean DeSmet traveled up the Missouri and encountered Yanktons. The story of his occasional visits with Sioux people through the ensuing three decades has not been adequately prepared, but a sketch of his activities is available in Louis Pfaller's *Father DeSmet in Dakota* [148].

Other Jesuits moved out to carry on DeSmet's work, but their efforts have been described only in obscure publications. Another giant among Catholic evangelists appeared during the 1870s, however—the Benedictine Martin Marty—and his work has been recorded in Albert Kleber's *History of Saint Meinrad Archabbey* [106].

The efforts of mission work begun by DeSmet and Marty must be gleaned from several sources. Gerald W. Wolff's scholarly "Father Sylvester Eisenman and Marty Mission" [208] describes the establishment and early development of an important mission and boarding school by a Benedictine on the Yankton reservation. Louis J. Goll's *Jesuit Missions among the Sioux* [73] deals with the later work of Jesuits among the Tetons. Sister Mary Claudia Duratschek's *Crusading along Sioux Trails* [51] is an apologetic but interesting survey that sums up the contributions of Catholic missionaries who have worked among Sioux people.

Congregational and Presbyterian Missionaries

Five years before Father DeSmet's initial expedition up the Missouri, the brothers Samuel and Gideon Pond appeared at the mouth of the Minnesota River to initiate the work of the American Board of Commissioners for Foreign Missions among the Sioux. They, their associates Thomas Williamson and Stephen Return Riggs, and the progeny of Williamson and Riggs have either created or inspired the best literature on the work and observations of missionaries among the Sioux. Two descriptions of the first important American Board of Commissioners for Foreign Missions mission station have been published: Charles Marvin Gates's "The Lac Qui Parle Indian Mission" [70] and Donald Dean Parker's *Lac Qui Parle: Its Missionaries, Traders and Indians* [145]. Samuel William Pond prepared a valuable, though biased, narrative on Isanti culture in his "The Dakotas or Sioux Indians in Minnesota as They Were in 1834" [152]; and, he wrote about his experiences, and those of his brother, in *Two Volunteer Missionaries among the Dakotas* [151].

Stephen Return Riggs, principal scholar among the early American Board of Commissioners for Foreign Missions missionaries, also published two books to accomplish similar purposes. *Mary and I* [158] is an autobiography rich in personal observations about Sioux

culture; and *Tah-Koo Wah-Kań* [157] deals with the
work of the American Board among the Isanti tribes.
Unfortunately, neither Thomas Williamson nor his
son John took time from their work on the production
of bilingual literature and other evangelical and educational endeavors to write books, but John's daughter,
Winifred Barton, has written about her father's life in
the sentimental but fascinating *John P. Williamson* [12].
With all the faults it contains as historical literature, her
book is perhaps the most important written to date
about missionaries among the Sioux because of the
wide range of services John P. Williamson performed.
As the first White person born in Minnesota, he grew
up with Sioux people and understood their language
and proclivities as well as he knew those of his own
White parents. From the time he entered the mission
field in 1861 to his death in 1917, he was respected by
Indians and non-Indians alike for his integrity and tire-
less dedication. For Indian people around him, he
served not only as evangelist and educator, but also as
interpreter and general secretary.

Next to Williamson in importance among second-
generation American Board of Commissioners for
Foreign Missions workers was Alfred Riggs. The principal product of his life's work has been described by
Richard L. Guenther in "The Santee Normal Training
School" [76]—a vocational-religious boarding school
that enrolled youngsters from all Sioux tribes from
1870 to 1936. For a brief but valuable survey of the
contributions of all important American Board of

Commissioners for Foreign Missions representatives in Sioux country, the reader should examine Robert J. Creswell's *Among the Sioux* [36].

Episcopal Missionaries

Episcopalians came last among major mission groups that have worked among Sioux people. Like the others, they were dedicated to the cause of cultural change; and, like the others they also worked with sincerity and integrity, more through institutional education than through personal evangelism. Foremost among them was Bishop Whipple, whose efforts are described in "The Work of Bishop Whipple in Missions for the Indians" [65] by Charles Eugene Flandreau. Next came William H. Hare, who served as Bishop of Niobrara from his arrival in the 1870s to his death in 1909. His life story has been recorded in *The Life and Labors of Bishop Hare* [88], by Marcus Antony DeWolfe Howe. The efforts of these two leaders, and of the many clergymen who worked with them late in the nineteenth century, are described in "The Episcopal Mission to the Dakotas" [209] by K. Brent Woodruff.

Captives

One other group of observers that recorded personal experiences of interest to general readers included persons who fell captive during hostilities.

Although their narratives reflect extreme anti-Indian bias caused by fright and anger and therefore should be approached with appropriate suspicion, they communicate important information. Most of them have become available in the Garland Library of *Narratives of North American Indian Captivities,* edited by Wilcomb E. Washburn [202].

Special Sioux Groups

Because Assiniboines and Canadian Sioux have long been separated from the rest of the Sioux, they have inspired few books and articles about their own histories. Only half a dozen publications have appeared on the Assiniboines. Edwin Thompson Denig's *Five Indian Tribes of the Upper Missouri* [43] contains a chapter on their condition in the nineteenth century. Dan Kennedy's *Recollections of an Assiniboine Chief* [104] is a collection of reminiscences and legends gathered in personal interviews by James R. Stevens. Robert H. Lowie's "The Assiniboine" [114] is an ethnology based upon Lowie's research in the years 1907–8 at Morley, Alberta, and Fort Belknap, Montana, which contains information about cultural habits, religion, and folklore. David Rodnick's "The Fort Belknap Assiniboine of Montana" [164] supplies some tribal history, a description of precontact life-style, and an assessment of recent conditions faced by one Assiniboine group. Chief John Snow's *The Mountains Are Our Sacred Places* [175], prepared by a political leader and clergyman of the tribe from personal interviews and documentary research, emphasizes the survival of Assiniboine culture in defiance of White accultura-tionists. A Montana Writers' Program publication, *The Assiniboines* [211], records tribal legends, games, hunting techniques, and ceremonies in addition to the effects of recent contacts with non-Indians.

The Canadian Sioux have been the subjects of even fewer sources. Gontran Laviolette's *The Sioux Indians of Canada* [111] is a scanty survey of their history down to the World War II period. Roy W. Meyer's "The Canadian Sioux: Refugees from Minnesota" [129] deals with the Isantis only to the end of the nineteenth century. Wilson Dallam Wallis's *The Canadian Dakotas* [201] appraises material culture, political organization, and social habits. Wallis's "Beliefs and Tales of the Canadian Dakota" [200] preserves stories he collected at Portage la Prairie and Griswold.

Culture

General Studies

Despite attacks against Sioux culture by agents, missionaries, teachers, and other non-Indians, as well as the acceptance of acculturation by "progressive" tribal members, Sioux "traditionalists" have preserved many legacies handed down to them from prehistory. Dartmouth-educated Charles Alexander Eastman was first among Indian authors to record the legacies in literature. In *Indian Boyhood* [53], *From the Deep Woods to Civilization* [57], and *Old Indian Days* [54], he wrote about habits and inclinations he had experienced while a youngster. In *The Indian Today* [56], he described the condition of Sioux culture after forty years of exposure to attack and ridicule. After Eastman, Carlisle-graduate Luther Standing Bear wrote from personal experience as he described similar traditions in *My People the Sioux* [177] and *Land of the Spotted Eagle* [179]. Subsequently, anthropologist Ella Cara Deloria recorded Sioux philosophy and folklore with help from reservation residents in *Speaking of Indians* [40].

Even more non-Indian authors have been attracted by these ancient legacies. In *Sioux Trail* [185], John Upton Terrell described the condition of the Sioux as the federation emerged "from the haze of antiquity." With *The Dakota or Sioux Indians* [86], James Henri Howard discussed the emergence of three cultural components as the Sioux made their adjustment to life on the prairies and the Great Plains during the second half of the eighteenth century. In "Anthropological Report . . . Dakota Sioux Indians" [91], Wesley Robert Hurt traced the development of one of these components down to the middle of the nineteenth century, and in *These Were the Sioux* [168], Mari Sandoz wrote about the habits of Teton people she knew in western Nebraska during the early part of the twentieth century.

In recent years, Royal B. Hassrick has published *The Sioux: Life and Customs of a Warrior Society* [80]. Robert H. Lowie has produced *Indians of the Plains* [116], which contains narratives on Sioux customs and arts. Ethel Nurge has edited the excellent anthology *The Modern Sioux* [138], which comprises eleven essays on the condition of reservation culture at the outset of the 1970s. Several writers have produced publications that focus attention upon single dimensions of Sioux culture. James Owen Dorsey's "Siouan Sociology" [49] reveals the social organization of the federation as its author observed it late in the nineteenth century. Ruth Landes's *The Mystic Lake Sioux* [108] is about the sociology of Mdewakantons on Prairie Island Reservation. John Francis Bryde's *Modern Indian Psychology* [23] appraises concepts and values of the Oglalas, among whom its author worked as a missionary for more than two decades. Melvin Randolph Gilmore's "Uses of Plants" [71] deals with the use of natural materials by tribes along the Missouri, and James Austin Hanson's *Metal Weapons, Tools and Ornaments of the Teton Dakota Indians* [78] probes the history of Teton material culture.

Language

Since the Pond brothers, Thomas Williamson, and Stephen Riggs teamed with Joseph Renville during the late 1830s and early 1840s to translate Scripture into Sioux language, numerous explanatory essays, word lists, dictionaries, grammars, and readers have appeared. James Owen Dorsey's "On the Comparative Phonology of Four Siouan Languages" [47] identifies the four dialects as Isanti, Yankton, Teton, and

Assiniboine and defines their phonetic differences. John P. Williamson's *English-Dakota Dictionary* [206], prepared for the eastern dialect, and Riggs's *Grammar and Dictionary of the Dakota Language* [161] and *Dakota Grammar, Texts, and Ethnography* [159]—also prepared for Isantis—are the oldest dictionaries in print. Eugene Buechel's *Grammar of Lakota* [25] and *Dictionary of the Teton Dakota Sioux Language* [26], in Teton dialect, have been made widely available since World War II.

In addition to these standard words, Ella Cara Deloria has prepared *Dakota Grammar* [18], assisting Franz Boas. Paul War Cloud Grant has written *Sioux Dictionary* [74], a list of four thousand common words with guides to pronunciation. LeRoy Hairy Shirt has compiled *Lakota Woonspe Wowapi* [77], an aid for non–Lakota–speaking Teton students, and Norman Balfour Levin has written *The Assiniboine Language* [113], the only publication on the Assiniboine dialect. No one has attempted a dictionary or grammar in Yankton, or "Nakota," dialect.

Religion

For all the publicity given the traditional religion of the Sioux, first because of attempts to extinguish it and later owing to a resurgence of interest in it, curious readers must gather bits of information from impressionistic literature that fails to explain either the philosophies upon which it is based or the liturgies and paraphernalia used by practitioners. Charles Alexander Eastman recorded his views on the philosophies of

Sioux religion in *The Soul of the Indian* [55]. Black Elk shared his experiences as a holy man with John Neihardt for the publication of *Black Elk Speaks* [15], and his impression of the seven rites of the Peacepipe with Joseph Brown for *The Sacred Pipe* [16]. Recently, medicineman John Fire shared similar information with Richard Erdoes for the production of *Lame Deer: Seeker of Visions* [63]. All these books make interesting reading, but none of them translates the ideas undergirding the Peacepipe Religion into terms understandable to non-Indians.

Earlier publications are even less instructive. James William Lynd's "Religion of the Dakotas" [118], prepared by a knowledgeable observer shortly before he died during the Minnesota Sioux War, is superficial in its treatment of philosophy. It is most valuable for being the first printed record of the practice of the famous *Yuwipi* ceremony. Out of half a dozen articles written by ethnologist Alice Cunningham Fletcher during her travels in the 1880s, "Indian Ceremonies" [66] and "The Sun Dance of the Ogalalla Sioux" [67] are the best, but they accomplish little beyond description of ceremonial equipment. James Owen Dorsey's article "A Study of Siouan Cults" [48] is useful only because it explains religious philosophy as a tonic for the problems of secular life.

Two other publications merit attention. James Mooney's "The Ghost Dance Religion and the Sioux Outbreak of 1890" [135] is a classic on the messianic movement imported from the Interior Basin that precipitated the massacre at Wounded Knee, and William K. Powers's *Oglala Religion* [154] shows how religious commitment has influenced the survival of ethnicity among traditionalists on Pine Ridge Reservation. Readers should not be discouraged from reviewing this literature, but they should realize that it neither explains the fundamental assumptions upon which traditional Sioux religion is based nor reveals the essential experiences of practitioners of the ancient faith.

Legends

Books and articles on Sioux legends are more understandable. Indeed, some of the those prepared by Indian authors are excellent. Charles Alexander and Elaine Goodale Eastman's *Wigwam Evenings* [58] is a collection of Isanti stories published for school and fireside reading by children. Marie L. McLaughlin's *Myths and Legends of the Sioux* [126] contains tales that the agent's wife remembered from her childhood in Wabasha, Minnesota. Ella Cara Deloria's *Dakota Texts* [39] comprises sixty-four stories supplied by traditionalists on Standing Rock, Pine Ridge, and Rosebud reservations. Luther Standing Bear's *Stories of the Sioux* [180] preserves legends used by Teton people both to entertain and to preserve knowledge about historical events, and James LaPointe's *Legends of the Lakota* [109] has been prepared recently for the education of young people.

Publications by non-Indians are less exciting, largely because they lack theme or specific purpose, but they also provide insight into Sioux culture. Those with most lasting value include: *Dahcotah* [59], by Mary Henderson Eastman; "Mythology of the Oglala Dakota" [13], thirty-seven stories collected by Martha Warren Beckwith; *Legends of the Mighty Sioux* [212], forty tales assembled by the South Dakota Writers' Program that have been reprinted for commercial distribution; and *Buckskin Tokens* [187], collected and edited by Ron D. Theisz on Rosebud Reservation.

Other Cultural Material

Published material on fine arts is scarce, even though Sioux music, dance, painting, and quill work can be traced back to prehistoric times. The most widely practiced art form is the composition of music and song lyrics, but only two scholars have collected and interpreted them for publication. The sensitive Frances Densmore wrote *Poems from Sioux and Chippewa Songs* [44] and *Teton Sioux Music* [45]. Harry W. Paige published *Songs of the Teton Sioux* [144], in which he revealed the origin, significance, and purpose of songs in western Sioux culture.

Sioux dance is a subject in two significant books. Robert H. Lowie's "Dance Associations of the Eastern Dakota" [115] explains procedures for eighteen dances and comments upon their social meaning. Reginald and Gladys Laubin's recent publication, *Indian Dances of North America* [110], is a description of the history and importance of dance among Indian people by two persons who are expert in the practice of the art.

Three scarce but important publications deal with the development of painting among the Sioux. Hartley Burr Alexander's *Sioux Indian Painting* [2] contains several Sioux paintings, along with those by other Great Plains artists. John Ronald Milton's *Oscar Howe: Artist* [133] is a collection of seventeen prints of the distinguished artist's original oils, with explanations of the cultural ideas they express. *Contemporary Sioux Painting* [191], produced under the aegis of the United States Indian Arts and Crafts Board, surveys and evaluates painting done by artists of Sioux extraction from 1900 to 1970. For information about crafts, a reader should see Carrie Alberta Lyford's *Quill and Bead Work of the Western Sioux* [117]. For descriptions of leisure-time activity, one should read James R. Walker's "Sioux Games" [198].

ALPHABETICAL LIST AND INDEX

*Denotes items suitable for secondary school students

Dakota Historical Collections 6:229–72,
1912; New Haven: Research Publica-
tions, 1975.   (6)

[5]   Ambrose, Stephen E. 1975. *Crazy Horse
and Custer: The Parallel Lives of Two
American Warriors.* New York: Double-
day.   (7)

[6]   Anderson, Harry H. 1973. "Fur Traders as Fathers: The Origins of the
Mixed-Blooded Community among the
Rosebud Sioux." *South Dakota History*
3:233–70.   (4)

[7]*   Anderson, John Alvin. 1971. *The Sioux
of the Rosebud: A History in Pictures.*
Norman: University of Oklahoma
Press.   (3)

[8]*   Andrist, Ralph K. 1964. *The Long Death;
The Last Days of The Plains Indian.* New
York: Macmillan. Reprinted, N.Y.: Col-
lier, 1969.   (12)

[9]   Artichoker, John, Jr., and Neil M.
Palmer. 1959. *The Sioux Indian Goes to*

College; an Analysis of Selected Problems of South Dakota Indian College Students. Vermillion, S.D.: Institute of Indian Studies. (21)

[10] Athearn, Robert. G. 1967. *Forts of the Upper Missouri.* Englewood Cliffs, N.J.: Prentice Hall. (20)

[11]* Bad Heart Bull, Amos. 1967. *A Pictographic History of the Oglala Sioux.* Text by Helen H. Blish. Intro. by Mari Sandoz. Lincoln: University of Nebraska Press. (3)

[12]* Barton, Winifred [Williamson]. 1919. *John P. Williamson: Brother of the Sioux.* New York: Fleming H. Revell. (26)

[13] Beckwith, Martha Warren. 1930. "Mythology of the Oglala Dakota." *Journal of American Folk-Lore* 43:339–442. (35)

[14] Berghold, Rev. Alexander, 1891. *The Indians' Revenge; or Days of Horror. Some Appalling Events in the History of the Sioux.* San Francisco: P. J. Thomas. Re-

printed, New Ulm, Minn.: Elroy E. Ubl
and MMI Graphics, 1976.   (12)

[15]*   Black. Elk. 1932. *Black Elk Speaks; Being
the Life Story of a Holy Man of the Oglala
Sioux as told to John G. Neihardt (Flaming
Rainbow).* Illus. by Standing Bear. New
York: W. Morrow. Reprinted, Lincoln:
University of Nebraska Press, 1961;
New York: Pocket Books, 1972.   (33)

[16]   ———. 1953. *The Sacred Pipe; Black
Elk's Account of the Seven Rites of the Og-
lala Sioux.* Recorded and ed. Joseph
Epes Brown. Norman: University of
Oklahoma Press. Reprinted, Baltimore:
Penguin Books, 1971.   (33)

[17]*   Blackthunder, Elijah, et. al. 1971. *His-
tory of the Sisseton-Wahpeton Sioux Tribe.*
Sisseton, S.D.: Sisseton-Wahpeton Sioux
Tribe.   (2)

[18]   Boas, Franz, and Ella C. Deloria. 1941.
Dakota Grammar. 2d Memoir, Vol. 23 in
Memoirs of the National Academy of
Sciences. Washington, D. C.: Govern-
ment Printing Office. Reprinted, N.Y.:

AMS, 1976; Vermillion, S.D.: Dakota
Press, 1979.   (32)

[19]   Bray, Edmund C., and Martha Coleman
       Bray, eds. 1976. *Joseph N. Nicollet on the
       Plains and Prairies.* Saint Paul. Minn.:
       Minnesota Historical Society.   (23)

[20]   Brininstool, Earl Alonzo. 1949. *Crazy
       Horse: The Invincible Ogalalla Sioux Chief,
       the Inside Stories by Actual Observers of a
       Most Treacherous Deed against a Great In-
       dian Leader.* Los Angeles: Wetzel Pub-
       lishing Company.   (7)

[21]   Brown, Dee A. 1970. *Bury My Heart at
       Wounded Knee; An Indian History of the
       American West.* New York: Holt,
       Rinehart and Winston.   (12)

[22]   Bryde, John Francis. 1966. *The Sioux
       Indian Student: A Study of Scholastic Fail-
       ure and Personality Conflict.* Pine Ridge,
       S.D.: Holy Rosary Mission.   (21)

[23]   ———. 1971. *Modern Indian Psychology.*
       Vermillion, S. D.: Institute of Indian
       Studies.   (31)

[24]   Buck, Daniel. 1904. *Indian Outbreaks.*
        Mankato, Minn.: Daniel Buck. Re-
        printed, Minneapolis: Ross and Haines,
        1965.   (14)

[25]   Buechel, Eugene, S. J. 1939. *A Grammar
        of Lakota, the Language of the Teton Sioux
        Indians.* Saint Louis and Chicago: John
        S. Swift.   (32)

[26]   ———. 1970. *A Dictionary of the Teton
        Dakota Sioux Language; Lakota-English,
        English-Lakota, with Considerations Given
        to Yankton and Santee.* Pine Ridge, S. D.:
        Red Cloud Indian School, Holy Rosary
        Mission.   (32)

[27]   Burdick, Usher Lloyd. 1940. *Tales from
        Buffalo Land; The Story of Fort Buford.*
        Baltimore: Wirth Brothers.   (6)

[28]   ———. 1941. *The Last Days of Sitting
        Bull, Sioux Medicine Chief.* Baltimore:
        Wirth Brothers.   (7)

[29]   Burnette, Robert. 1971. *The Tortured
        Americans.* Englewood Cliffs, N.J.:
        Prentice-Hall.   (19)

[30]   Carley, Kenneth A., ed. 1962. "As Red
         Men Viewed It: Three Indian Accounts
         of the Uprising." *Minnesota History*
         38:126–49.   (15)

[31]*   Cash, Joseph H. 1971. *The Sioux People
         (Rosebud)*. Phoenix: Indian Tribal
         Series.   (2)

[32]*   Cash, Joseph H., and Herbert T.
         Hoover, eds. 1971. *To Be An Indian; An
         Oral History*. New York: Holt, Rinehart
         and Winston.   (21)

[33]   Catlin, George. 1841. *Letters and Notes
         on the Manners, Customs, and Conditions of
         the North American Indians*. New York:
         Wiley and Putnam. Published the same
         year in London by the author. Re-
         printed in many editions. Most accessi-
         ble, New York: Dover, 1973.   (23)

[34]   Clark, Robert A., ed. 1976. *The Killing
         of Chief Crazy Horse: Three Eyewitness
         Views by the Indian Chief He Dog, the
         Indian-White William Garnett, the White
         Doctor Valentine McGillycuddy*. Glendale:
         Arthur H. Clark.   (7)

[35]   Coues, Elliott, ed. 1895. *The Expeditions of Zebulon Montgomery Pike to Headwaters of the Mississippi River, through Louisiana Territory, and in New Spain, During the Years 1805–6–7.* 3 vols. New York: Francis P. Harper. Reprinted, Minneapolis: Ross and Haines, 1965.   (22)

[36]   Creswell, Rev. Robert J. 1906. *Among the Sioux: A Story of the Twin Cities and the Two Dakotas,* intro. Rev. David R. Breed. Minneapolis: University Press.   (27)

[37]   Daniels, Asa W. 1908. "Reminiscences of Little Crow." *Collections of the Minnesota Historical Society* 12:513–30.   (8)

[38]   ———. 1915. "Reminiscences of the Little Crow Uprising." *Collections of the Minnesota Historical Society* 15:323–36.   (14)

[39]   Deloria, Ella C. 1932. *Dakota Texts.* New York: G. E. Stechert. Reprinted, Vermillion, S.D.: Dakota Press, 1978.   (34)

[40]   ———. 1944. *Speaking of Indians.* New York: Friendship Press. Reprinted, Vermillion, S.D.: Dakota Press, 1978.   (30)

[41]   Deloria, Vine, Jr. 1969. *Custer Died for Your Sins: An Indian Manifesto.* New York: Macmillan. Reprinted, New York: Avon Books, 1970.   (19)

[42]   ———. 1974. *Behind the Trail of Broken Treaties: An Indian Declaration of Independence.* New York: Delacorte.   (19)

[43]*   Denig, Edwin Thompson. 1961. *Five Indian Tribes of the Upper Missouri: Sioux, Arikaras, Assiniboines, Crees, Crows,* intro. and ed. John C. Ewers. Norman: University of Oklahoma Press.   (23, 28)

[44]   Densmore, Frances. 1917. *Poems from Sioux and Chippewa Songs.* Washington, D.C.: n.p.   (35)

[45]   ———. 1918. *Teton Sioux Music.* Bureau of American Ethnology *Bulletin 61.* Washington, D. C.: Government Printing Office. Reprinted, New York: Da Capo, 1972.   (35)

[46]   Diehl, Charles. 1912. "Crazy Horse's Story of the Custer Battle." *South Dakota Historical Collections* 6:224–28.   (7)

[47]   Dorsey, Rev. James Owen. 1885. "On the Comparative Phonology of Four Siouan Languages." In *Annual Report of the Smithsonian Institution, 1883*, pp. 919–29. Washington, D.C.: Government Printing Office.   (31)

[48]   ———. 1894. "A Study of Siouan Cults." In *Eleventh Annual Report of the United States Bureau of American Ethnology*, pp. 351–544. Washington, D.C.: Government Printing Office.   (33)

[49]   ———. 1897. "Siouan Sociology." In *Fifteenth Annual Report of the United States Bureau of American Ethnology*, pp. 205–44. Washington, D.C.: Government Printing Office.   (31)

[50]   Drum, Gen. Richard C. 1911. "Reminiscences of the Indian Fight at Ash Hollow, 1855." *Nebraska State Historical Society Collections*. 16:143–51.   (12)

[51]   Duratschek, Sister Mary Claudia. 1947. *Crusading along Sioux Trails: A History of the Catholic Indian Missions of South Dakota*. Saint Meinrad, Indiana: Grail Publishers.   (24)

[52]* Dyck, Paul. 1971. *Brule: The Sioux People of Rosebud.* Flagstaff, Arizona: Northland Press. (3)

[53] Eastman, Charles Alexander. 1902. *Indian Boyhood.* New York: McClure, Phillips. Reprinted, Glorieta, New Mexico: Rio Grande Press, 1976. (9, 29)

[54]* ———. 1907. *Old Indian Days.* New York: McClure. Reprinted, Rapid City, S.D.: Fenwyn Press, 1970. (29)

[55]* ———. 1911. *The Soul of the Indian: An Interpretation.* Boston and New York: Houghton Mifflin. Reprinted, New York: Johnson, 1971. (33)

[56] ———. 1915. *The Indian Today: The Past and Future of the First American.* New York: Doubleday, Page, Reprinted, New York: AMS, 1975. (29)

[57]* ———. 1916. *From the Deep Woods to Civilization: Chapters in the Autobiography of an Indian.* Boston: Little, Brown. Reprinted, Lincoln: University of Nebraska Press, 1977. (10, 29)

[58]   Eastman, Charles Alexander, and Elaine Goodale Eastman. 1909. *Wigwam Evenings: Sioux Folk Tales Retold.* Boston: Little, Brown. Reprinted, Eau Claire, Wisconsin: E. M. Hale, 1937.   (34)

[59]   Eastman, Mary Henderson. 1849. *Dahcotah; or Life and Legends of the Sioux around Fort Snelling.* New York: John Wiley. Reprinted, Minneapolis: Ross and Haines, 1962; New York: Arno, 1975.   (35)

[60]   Fay, George E., ed. 1972. *Treaties and Land Cessions between the Bands of the Sioux and the United States of America, 1805–1906.* Greeley, Colorado: University of Northern Colorado Museum of Anthropology.   (18)

[61]   Fechet, Col. Edmond Gustav. 1908. "The Capture of Sitting Bull." *South Dakota Historical Collections* 4:185–93.   (6)

[62]   Finerty, John Frederick. 1890. *War-Path and Bivouac; or, The Conquest of the Sioux, a Narrative of Stirring Personal Experiences and Adventures in the Big Horn and*

Yellowstone Expedition of 1876 and in the Campaign on the British Border in 1879. Chicago: Donohue and Henneberry. Reprinted, Chicago: R. R. Donnelley, 1955; Norman: University of Oklahoma Press, 1961. (16)

[63] Fire, John (Lame Deer), and Richard Erdoes. 1972. *Lame Deer: Seeker of Visions.* New York: Simon and Schuster. Reprinted, New York: Pocket Books, 1978. (33)

[64] Flandreau, Charles Eugene. 1880. "The Ink-pa-du-ta Massacre of 1857." *Collections of the Minnesota Historical Society* 3:386–407. (13)

[65] ———. 1905. "The Work of Bishop Whipple in Missions for the Indians." *Collections of the Minnesota Historical Society,* 10, part 2:691–96. (27)

[66] Fletcher, Alice Cunningham. 1883. "Indian Ceremonies." *Report of the Museum of American Archaeology and Ethnology* 16:260–333. (33)

[67]   ———. 1883. "The Sun Dance of the Ogalalla Sioux." *Proceedings of the American Association for the Advancement of Science* 31:580–84.   (33)

[68]   Garst, Doris Shannon. 1946. *Sitting Bull: Champion of His People.* New York: Julian Messner.   (6)

[69]   ———. 1950. *Crazy Horse: A Great Warrior of the Sioux.* Boston and New York: Houghton Mifflin.   (7)

[70]   Gates, Charles Marvin. 1935. "The Lac Qui Parle Indian Mission." *Minnesota History* 16:133–51.   (25)

[71]   Gilmore, Melvin Randolph. 1919. "Uses of Plants by the Indians of the Missouri River Region." *Thirty-third Annual Report of the United States Bureau of American Ethnology,* part 1, pp. 45–154. Washington, D.C.: Government Printing Office. Reprinted with foreward by Hugh Cutler, Lincoln: University of Nebraska Press, 1977.   (31)

[72] Gluek, Alvin C., Jr. 1955. "The Sioux Uprising: A Problem in International Relations." *Minnesota History* 34:317–24. (16)

[73] Goll, Louis J., S. J. 1940. *Jesuit Missions among the Sioux*. Saint Francis, S.D.: Saint Francis Mission. (24)

[74] Grant, Paul War Cloud. 1971. *Sioux Dictionary: Over 4,000 Words, Pronunciation at-a-Glance*. Pierre, S.D.: State Publishing Company. (32)

[75] Gray, John S. 1976. *Centennial Campaign: The Sioux War of 1876*, maps by John A. Popovich. Fort Collins, Colorado: Old Army Press. (16)

[76] Guenther, Richard L. 1970. "The Santee Normal Training School." *Nebraska History* 51:359–78. (26)

[77] Hairy Shirt, LeRoy, et al. 1973. *Lakota Woonspe Wowapi*. Rosebud, S.D.: Sinte Gleske College. (32)

[78]   Hanson, James Austin. 1975. *Metal Weapons, Tools and Ornaments of the Teton Dakota Indians.* Lincoln: University of Nebraska Press.   (31)

[79]   Harkins, Arthur M., et al. 1969 *Public Education of the Prairie Island Sioux: An Interim Report.* Minneapolis: University of Minnesota.   (22)

[80]   Hassrick, Royal B., Dorothy Maxwell and Cile M. Bach. 1964. *The Sioux: Life and Customs of a Warrior Society.* Norman: University of Oklahoma Press.   (30)

[81]   Heard, Isaac V. D. 1863. *History of the Sioux War and Massacres of 1862 and 1863.* New York: Harper. Reprinted, Millwood, New York: Kraus, 1975.   (13)

[82]   Hennepin, Louis, O. S. F. 1698. *A New Discovery of a Vast Country in America, extending above Four Thousand Miles, between New France and New Mexico; with a Description of the Great Lakes, Cataracts, Rivers, Plants, and Animals. Also, the Manners, Customs and Languages of the Several Native Indians; and the Advantages*

of Commerce with those Different Nations. London: Printed for M. Bentley, J. Tonfon, H. Bonwick, et al. Reprinted, Chicago: A. C. McClurg, 1903; Millwood, New York: Kraus, 1972; Toronto: Coles Publishing Co., 1974. (23)

[83] Hickerson, Harold. 1974. "Mdewakanton Band of Sioux Indians: An Anthropological Report on the Indian Occupancy of Area 243 and Area 289." American Indian Ethnohistory Series: Plains Indians. *Sioux Indians,* vol. 1. New York: Garland. (1)

[84] Hoopes, Alban Williamson. 1975. *The Road to the Little Big Horn —and Beyond.* New York: Vantage Press. (12)

[85] Hoover, Herbert T. 1976. "Yankton Sioux Tribal Claims Against the United States, 1917– 1975." *Western Historical Quarterly* 7:125– 42. (21)

[86]* Howard, James Henri. 1966. *The Dakota or Sioux Indians.* Vermillion, S.D.: Dakota Museum. (30)

[87]   ———, trans. and ed. 1968. *The Warrior Who Killed Custer: The Personal Narrative of Chief Joseph White Bull.* Lincoln: University of Nebraska Press.   (9)

[88]   Howe, Marcus Antony De Wolfe. 1911. *The Life and Labors of Bishop Hare, Apostle to the Sioux.* New York: Sturgis and Walton.   (27)

[89]   Hughes, Thomas. 1908. "Causes and Results of the Inkpaduta Massacre." *Collections of the Minnesota Historical Society* 12:263–82.   (13)

[90]   ———. 1927. *Indian Chiefs of Southern Minnesota: Containing Sketches of the Prominent Chieftains of the Dakota and Winnebago Tribes from 1825 to 1865.* Mankato, Minn.: Free Press. Reprinted, Minneapolis: Ross and Haines, 1969.   (10)

[91]   Hurt, Wesley Robert. 1974. "Anthropological Report on Indian Occupancy of Certain Territory Claimed by the Dakota Sioux Indians and by Rival Tribal Claimants." American Indian Ethnohistory Series: Plains Indians.

Sioux Indians, vol. 2. New York: Garland. (30)

[92] Hyde, George E. 1937. *Red Cloud's Folk: A History of the Oglala Sioux Indians.* Norman: University of Oklahoma Press. (1, 8)

[93] ———. 1956. *A Sioux Chronicle.* Norman: University of Oklahoma Press. (1, 8)

[94] ———. 1961. *Spotted Tail's Folk: A History of the Brule Sioux.* Norman: University of Oklahoma Press. (1)

[95] Innis, Ben. 1973. *Bloody Knife: Custer's Favorite Scout.* Fort Collins, Colorado: Old Army Press. (9)

[96] Jackson, Donald D. 1966. *Custer's Gold: The United States Cavalry Expedition of 1874.* New Haven: Yale University Press. Reprinted, Lincoln: University of Nebraska Press, 1972. (16)

[97]   Johnson, Dorothy M. 1969. *Warrior for a Lost Nation: A Biography of Sitting Bull.* Philadelphia: Westminster Press.   (6)

[98]   Johnson, Willis Fletcher. 1891. *The Red Record of the Sioux: Life of Sitting Bull and History of the Indian War of 1890–91.* Philadelphia: Edgewood Publishing Company.   (5)

[99]   Johnston, Sister Mary Antonio. 1948. *Federal Relations with the Great Sioux Indians of South Dakota, 1887–1933, with Particular Reference to Land Policy under the Dawes Act.* Washington, D.C.: Catholic University of America Press.   (21)

[100]   Jones, Robert Huhn. 1960. *The Civil War in the Northwest: Nebraska, Wisconsin, Iowa, Minnesota, and the Dakotas.* Norman: University of Oklahoma Press.   (15)

[101]*   Josephy, Alvin M., Jr. 1961. *The Patriot Chiefs: A Chronicle of American Indian Leadership.* New York: Viking Press. New ed., 1976.   (7)

[102]   Kappler, Charles J., comp. 1903– 41.
Indian Affairs, Laws and Treaties. 5 vols.
Washington, D.C.: Government Printing
Office. Vol. 2, *Treaties,* 1904. Senate
Document no. 319, 59th Congress, 2d
sess., serial no. 4624. Reprinted, New
York: Interland, 1972.   (18)

[103]   Kelley, William Fitch. 1971. *Pine Ridge,
1890: An Eye Witness Account of the
Events Surrounding the Fighting at
Wounded Knee,* ed. and comp. Alexander Kelley and Pierre Bovis. San Francisco: P. Bovis. Originally published in
Nebraska State Journal, 1– 24 November,
1890; 16 January, 1891.   (17)

[104]   Kennedy, Dan (Ochankugahe). 1972.
Recollections of an Assiniboine Chief, intro.
and ed. James R. Stevens. Toronto:
McClelland and Stewart.   (28)

[105]   Kingsbury, David L. 1898. "Sully's Expedition against the Sioux in 1864." *Collections of the Minnesota Historical Society*
8:449– 62.   (15)

[106] Kleber, Albert, O. S. B. 1954. *History of Saint Meinrad Archabbey, 1854–1954.* Saint Meinrad, Ind.: Grail Press.   (24)

[107] Kutzlieb, Charles R. 1965. "Educating the Sioux, 1876–1890." *North Dakota History* 32:197–216.   (21)

[108] Landes, Ruth. 1968. *The Mystic Lake Sioux: Sociology of the Mdewakantonwan Santee.* Madison: University of Wisconsin Press.   (31)

[109]* LaPointe, James. 1975. *Legends of the Lakota,* illustr. Louis Amiotte. San Francisco: Indian Historian Press.   (34)

[110] Laubin, Reginald, and Gladys Laubin. 1977. *Indian Dances of North America: Their Importance to Indian Life.* Norman: University of Oklahoma Press.   (35)

[111] Laviolette, Gontran, O.M.I. 1944. *The Sioux Indians of Canada.* Regina, Sask.: Marian Press.   (28)

[112]   Lee, Lorenzo Porter. 1857. *History of the Spirit Lake Massacre: 8th March, 1857, and of Miss Abigail Gardner's Three Months Captivity among the Indians According to Her Own Account, as Given to L. P. Lee.* New Britain, Conn.: L. P. Lee. Reprinted, Fairfield, Wash.: Ye Galleon Press, 1967.   (13)

[113]   Levin, Norman Balfour. 1964. *The Assiniboine Language.* Bloomington: Indiana University Press.   (32)

[114]   Lowie, Robert H. 1909. "The Assiniboine." *Anthropological Papers of the Museum of Natural History* 4, part 1:1–270. New York: The Trustees of the Museum. Reprinted, New York: AMS, 1975.   (28)

[115]   ———. 1913. "Dance Associations of the Eastern Dakota." *Anthropological Papers of the Museum of Natural History,* 11, part 2:101–42. New York: The Trustees of the Museum.   (35)

[116]*   ———. 1954. *Indians of the Plains.* New York: McGraw-Hill. Published for the

Museum of Natural History. Anthropological Handbook No. 1. Reprinted, Garden City: Natural History Press, 1963.   (30)

[117]   Lyford, Carrie Alberta. 1940. *Quill and Bead Work of the Western Sioux.* Willard W. Beatty, ed. Lawrence, Kansas: Haskell Institute. A publication of the Education Division, United States Office of Indian Affairs.   (36)

[118]   Lynd, James William. 1864. "Religion of the Dakotas." *Collections of the Minnesota Historical Society* 2:150–74.   (33)

[119]   McConkey, Harriet E. Bishop. 1863. *Dakota War Whoop; or, Indian Massacres and War in Minnesota of 1862–63.* Saint Paul, Minn.: D. D. Merrill. Reprinted, Minneapolis: Ross and Haines, 1970.   (13)

[120]*   MacEwan, John Walter Grant. 1973. *Sitting Bull: The Years in Canada.* Edmonton, Alberta: Hurtig Publishers.   (6)

[121]   McGillycuddy, Julia Blanchard. 1941. *McGillycuddy, Agent: A Biography of Dr.*

Valentine T. McGillycuddy. Palo Alto: Stanford University Press. (20)

[122] Macgregor, Gordon. 1946. *Warriors without Weapons: A Study of the Society and Personality Development of the Pine Ridge Sioux.* Chicago: University of Chicago Press. (3)

[123] McGregor, James Herman. 1940. *The Wounded Knee Massacre from the Viewpoint of the Sioux.* Baltimore: Wirth Brothers. (17)

[124] McKenney, Thomas L, and James Hall. 1838–44. *History of the Indian Tribes of North America, with Biographical Sketches and Anecdotes of the Principal Chiefs, Embellished with One Hundred and Twenty Portraits from the Indian Gallery in the Department of War, at Washington.* 3 vols. Philadelphia: Frederick W. Greenough. New ed., ed. Frederick W. Hodge, Edinburgh: J. Grant, 1933–34. (10)

[125] McLaughlin, Maj. James. 1910. *My Friend the Indian.* Boston and New York: Houghton Mifflin. Reprinted as *The*

Superior Edition of My Friend the Indian, preface and epilogue by Rev. Louis L. Pfaller, O.S.B. Seattle: Superior Publishing Company, 1970.   (6, 20)

[126]   McLaughlin, Marie L. 1916. *Myths and Legends of the Sioux.* Bismarck, N.D.: Bismarck Tribune.   (34)

[127]   Maynard, Eileen, and Gayla Twiss. 1969. *That these People May Live.* Pine Ridge, S.D.: United States Public Health Service Unit.   (4)

[128]   Meyer, Roy W. 1967. *History of the Santee Sioux: United States Indian Policy on Trial.* Lincoln: University of Nebraska Press.   (1)

[129]   ———. 1968. "The Canadian Sioux: Refugees from Minnesota." *Minnesota History* 41:13–28.   (29)

[130]   Milligan, Edward A. 1973. *Wounded Knee 1973 and the Fort Laramie Treaty of 1868.* Bottineau, N.D.: Bottineau Courant Print.   (18)

[131] ———. 1976. *Dakota Twilight: The Standing Rock Sioux, 1874–1890.* Hicksville, New York: Exposition Press. (2)

[132] Milton, John Ronald. 1971. *Oscar Howe: The Story of an American Indian.* Minneapolis: Dillon Press. (10)

[133] ———. 1974. *Oscar Howe: Artist.* Vermillion, S.D.: University of South Dakota Press. (36)

[134] Minnesota Board of Commissioners on Publication of the History of Minnesota in the Civil and Indian Wars. 1890–93. *Minnesota in the Civil and Indian Wars, 1861–1865.* 2 vols. Saint Paul: Pioneer Press. (14)

[135] Mooney, James. 1896. "The Ghost Dance Religion and the Sioux Outbreak of 1890." In *Fourteenth Annual Report of the United States Bureau of Ethnology,* pp. 641–1136. Washington, D.C.: Government Printing Office. Reprinted, Chicago: University of Chicago Press, 1965. (33)

[136]   Nadeau, Remi A. 1967. *Fort Laramie and the Sioux Indians*. Englewood Cliffs, N.J.: Prentice-Hall.   (3)

[137]   National Indian Defense Association. 1891. *The Sioux Nation and the United States: A Brief History of the Treaties of 1868, 1876, and 1889 between That Nation and the United States*. Washington, D.C.: National Indian Defense Association.   (19)

[138]   Nurge, Ethel, ed. 1970. *The Modern Sioux: Social Systems and Reservation Culture*. Lincoln: University of Nebraska Press.   (31)

[139]*   O'Conner, Richard. 1968. *Sitting Bull: War Chief of the Sioux*. New York: McGraw-Hill.   (6)

[140]   Oehler, Charles M. 1959. *The Great Sioux Uprising*. New York: Oxford University Press.   (15)

[141]   Oglesby, Richard E. 1963. *Manuel Lisa and the Opening of the Missouri Fur Trade*.

Norman: University of Oklahoma
Press.   (22)

[142]* Olson, James C. 1965. *Red Cloud and the Sioux Problem.* Lincoln: University of Nebraska Press.   (1, 8)

[143] Ortiz, Roxanne Dunbar, ed. 1977. *The Great Sioux Nation: Sitting in Judgment on America.* Berkeley: Moon Books.   (19)

[144] Paige, Harry W. 1970. *Songs of the Teton Sioux.* Los Angeles: Westernlore Press.   (35)

[145] Parker, Donald Dean. 1964. *Lac Qui Parle: Its Missionaries, Traders and Indians.* Brookings, S.D.: Donald Dean Parker.   (25)

[146] Paulson, Howard W. 1973. "Federal Indian Policy and the Dakota Indians: 1800–1840." *South Dakota History* 3:285–309.   (19)

[147] Pennanen, Gary. 1970. "Sitting Bull: Indian Without a Country." *Canadian Historical Review* 51:123–40.   (6)

[148]   Pfaller, Louis, O.S.B. 1962. *Father De-Smet in Dakota.* Richardton, N.D.: Assumption Abbey Press.   (24)

[149]   ———. 1964. "Sully's Expedition of 1864: Featuring the Killdeer Mountain and Badlands Battles." *North Dakota History* 31:25–77.   (15)

[150]   Phillips, George H. 1972. "The Indian Ring in Dakota Territory, 1870–1890." *South Dakota History* 2:344–76.   (20)

[151]   Pond, Rev. Samuel William. 1893. *Two Volunteer Missionaries among the Dakotas; or The Story of the Labors of Samuel W. and Gideon Pond.* Boston: Congregational Sunday-School and Publishing Society.   (25)

[152]   ———. 1908. "The Dakotas or Sioux in Minnesota as They Were in 1834." *Collections of the Minnesota Historical Society* 12:319–501.   (25)

[153]   Poole, DeWitt Clinton, 1881. *Among the Sioux or Dakota: Eighteen Months Experi-*

ence as an Indian Agent. New York: Van
Nostrand. (20)

[154] Powers, William K. 1977. *Oglala Religion.* Lincoln: University of Nebraska
Press. (34)

[155] Prucha, Francis Paul, S.J. 1976. *American Indian Policy in Crisis: Christian Reformers and the Indian, 1865–1900.*
Norman: University of Oklahoma
Press. (20)

[156] Renville, Gabriel. 1905. "A Sioux Narrative of the Outbreak in 1862, and of
Sibley's Expedition in 1863 with a Biographical Sketch of the Author by
Samuel J. Brown." *Collections of the Minnesota Historical Society* 10, part 2:596–
618. (15)

[157] Riggs, Rev. Stephen Return. 1869.
*Tah-Koo Wah-Kań; or the Gospel among the
Dakotas,* intro. S. B. Treat. Boston:
Congregational Sabbath-School and
Publishing Society. Reprinted, New
York: Arno, 1972. (26)

[158]*   ———. 1880. *Mary and I: Forty Years with the Sioux.* Chicago: W. G. Holmes. Reprinted, Minneapolis: Ross and Haines, 1969.   (25)

[159]   ———. 1893. *Dakota Grammar, Texts, and Ethnography,* ed. James Owen Dorsey. Washington, D.C.: Government Printing Office. Reprinted, Marvin, S.D.: Blue Cloud Abbey, 1977.   (32)

[160]   ———. 1918. "Dakota Portraits." *Minnesota History Bulletin* 2:481–568.   (10)

[161]   ———. ed. 1852. *Grammar and Dictionary of the Dakota Language: Collected by Members of the Dakota Mission.* Published under the patronage of the Historical Society of Minnesota. Washington, D.C.: Smithsonian Institution Contributions to Knowledge, vol. 4. New York: G. P. Putnam.   (32)

[162]*   Robinson, Doane. 1904. *A History of the Dakota or Sioux Indians from Their Earliest Traditions and First Contact with White Men to the Final Settlement of the Last of Them upon Reservations and the Conse-*

quent *Abandonment of the Old Tribal Life.*
Originally published in *South Dakota
Historical Collections* 2:1–523. Reprinted, Minneapolis: Ross and Haines,
1974.   (1)

[163] Roddis, Louis Harry. 1956. *The Indian
Wars of Minnesota.* Cedar Rapids, Iowa:
Torch Press.   (14)

[164] Rodnick, David. 1938. "The Fort
Belknap Assiniboine of Montana: A
Study in Culture Change." Ph. D. diss.,
University of Pennsylvania.   (28)

[165] Ruby, Robert H. 1955. *The Oglala Sioux:
Warriors in Transition.* New York: Vantage Press.   (4)

[166] Sage, Walter N. 1935. "Sitting Bull's
Own Narrative of the Custer Fight."
Canadian Historical Review 16:170–76.   (6)

[167]* Sandoz, Mari. 1942. *Crazy Horse, the
Strange Man of the Oglalas: A Biography.*
New York: Alfred A. Knopf. Reprinted, Lincoln: University of Ne-
braska Press, 1961.   (7)

[168]*   ———. 1961. *These Were the Sioux*. New York: Hastings House. Reprinted, New York: Dell Publishing Company, 1971.   (30)

[169]*   ———. 1966. *The Battle of the Little Bighorn*. Philadelphia: J. B. Lippincott. Reprinted, Lincoln: University of Nebraska Press, 1978.   (16)

[170]   Sanford, Paul. 1969. *Sioux Arrows and Bullets*. San Antonio: Naylor.   (15)

[171]   Schusky, Ernest Lester. 1959. *Politics and Planning in a Dakota Indian Community: A Case Study of Views on Termination and Plans for Rehabilitation on the Lower Brule Reservation in South Dakota*. Vermillion, S.D.: Institute of Indian Studies.   (4)

[172]   ———. 1975. *The Forgotten Sioux: An Ethnohistory of the Lower Brule Reservation*. Chicago: Nelson-Hall.   (2)

[173]   Sibley, Henry Hastings. 1950. *Iron Face: The Adventures of Jack Frazer, Frontier Warrior, Scout, and Hunter*, intro, and

ed. Theodore C. Blegen and Sarah A. Davidson. Foreword by Stanley Vestal. Chicago: The Caxton Club. (9)

[174] Sneve, Virginia Driving Hawk. 1975. *They Led the Nation,* ed. N. Jane Hunt. Sioux Falls, S.D.: Brevet Press. (10)

[175] Snow, Chief John. 1977. *The Mountains Are Our Sacred Places: The Story of the Stoney Indians.* Toronto: Samuel Stevens. (28)

[176] Spindler, Will H. 1955. *Tragedy Strikes at Wounded Knee.* Gordon, Nebraska: Gordon Journal Publishing Company. Reprinted, Vermillion, S.D.: University of South Dakota Press, 1972. (17)

[177]* Standing Bear, Luther. 1928. *My People the Sioux,* ed. E. A. Brininstool. Boston and New York: Houghton Mifflin. Reprinted, Lincoln: University of Nebraska Press, 1975. (30)

[178]* ———. 1931. *My Indian Boyhood.* Boston and New York: Houghton Mifflin. (10)

[179]*   ———. 1933. *Land of the Spotted Eagle.* Boston and New York: Houghton Mifflin.   (30)

[180]*   ———. 1934. *Stories of the Sioux.* Boston and New York: Houghton Mifflin.   (34)

[181]   Stewart, Edgar Irving. 1955. *Custer's Luck.* Norman: University of Oklahoma Press.   (16)

[182]   Stirling, Matthew William. 1938. *Three Pictographic Autobiographies of Sitting Bull.* Washington, D.C.: Smithsonian Institution.   (5)

[183]   Taliaferro, Maj. Lawrence. 1894. "Autobiography of Maj. Lawrence Taliaferro, Indian Agent at Fort Snelling, 1820–1840." *Collections of the Minnesota Historical Society* 6:189–256.   (20)

[184]   Teakle, Thomas. 1918. *The Spirit Lake Massacre.* Iowa City: State Historical Society of Iowa.   (13)

[185]   Terrell, John Upton. 1974. *Sioux Trail.* New York: McGraw-Hill.   (30)

[186]   Textor, Lucy Elizabeth. 1896. *Official Relations between the United States and the Sioux Indians*. Leland Stanford, Jr. University Publications, History and Economics, no. 2. Palo Alto: Stanford University Press. (20)

[187]   Theisz, Ron D., ed. 1975. *Buckskin Tokens: Contemporary Oral Narratives of the Lakota*. Rosebud, S.D.: Sinte Gleska College. Distributed by North Plains Press. (35)

[188]   Thwaites, Reuben Gold, ed. 1896–1901. *The Jesuit Relations and Allied Documents; Travels and Explorations of the Jesuit Missionaries in New France, 1610–1791*. 73 vols. Cleveland: Burrows Brothers. Reprinted in 36 vols., New York: Pageant Book Company, 1959. (23)

[189]   ———. 1904–05. *Original Journals of the Lewis and Clark Expedition, 1804–06*. 8 vols. New York: Dodd, Mead. New ed., N. Y.: Antiquarian Press, 1959. New ed., with intro by Bernard DeVoto, New York: Arno, 1969. (22)

[190]*   United States Bureau of Indian Affairs. 1966. *Famous Indians: A Collection of*

Short Biographies. Washington, D.C.: Government Printing Office.   (10)

[191]   United States Indian Arts and Crafts Board. 1970. *Contemporary Sioux Painting: An Exhibition Organized by the Indian Arts and Crafts Board of the United States Department of the Interior.* Rapid City, S.D.: Tipi Shop.   (36)

[192]   United States Indian Claims Commission. 1974. "Commission Findings on the Sioux Indians." American Indian Ethnohistory Series: Plains Indians. *Sioux Indians,* vol. 4. New York: Garland. See [210] for vol. 3, "Ethnohistorical Report on the Yankton Sioux."   (21)

[193]   Utley, Robert M. 1963. *The Last Days of the Sioux Nation.* New Haven: Yale University Press.   (18)

[194]   ———. 1973. *Frontier Regulars: The United States Army and the Indian, 1866–1891.* New York: Macmillan. Reprinted, Bloomington: Indiana University Press, 1977.   (12)

[195]   Vaughn, Jesse Wendell. 1966. *Indian Fight: New Facts on Several Encounters.* Norman: University of Oklahoma Press.   (12)

[196]* Vestal, Stanley. 1932. *Sitting Bull: Champion of the Sioux; A Biography.* Boston and New York: Houghton Mifflin. New ed., Norman: University of Oklahoma Press, 1957. Reprinted, Norman: University of Oklahoma Press, 1972.   (5)

[197]* ———. 1934. *Warpath: The True Story of the Fighting Sioux Told in a Biography of Chief White Bull.* Boston and New York: Houghton Mifflin.   (9)

[198]* Walker, James R. 1918. "Sioux Games." *South Dakota Historical Collections* 9:486–513.   (36)

[199]   Wall, Oscar Garrett. 1909. *Recollections of the Sioux Massacre: An Authentic History of the Yellow Medicine Incident, of the Fate of Marsh and His Men, of the Siege and Battles of Fort Ridgely, and of Other Important Battles and Experiences, Together with a Historical Sketch of the Sibley Expedition*

of 1863. Lake City, Minn.: M. C. Russell.   (14)

[200]   Wallis, Wilson Dallam. 1923. "Beliefs and Tales of the Canadian Dakota." *Journal of American Folk-Lore* 36:36–101.   (29)

[201]   ———. 1947. *The Canadian Dakotas.* Anthropological Papers of the American Museum of Natural History, vol. 41, part 1.   (29)

[202]   Washburn, Wilcomb E., ed. 1977– *Narratives of North American Indian Captivities.* 111 vols. New York: Garland.   (28)

[203]   Wax, Murray Lionel, et. al. 1964. *Formal Education in an American Indian Community.* Advisors, Roselyn Holyrock and Gerald Onefeather. Atlanta: Emory University Press.   (22)

[204]   West, Nathaniel. 1889. *The Ancestry, Life and Times of Hon. Henry Hastings Sibley, LL.D.* Saint Paul, Minn.: Pioneer Press.   (15)

[205] White, Richard. 1978. "The Winning of the West: The Expansion of the Western Sioux in the Eighteenth and Nineteenth Centuries." *Journal of American History* 65, no. 2:319–43. (11)

[206] Williamson, Rev. John P. 1908. *An English-Dakota Dictionary: Wasicun ka Dakota leska Wowapi.* New York: American Tract Society. (32)

[207] Willson, Charles C. 1908. "The Successive Chiefs Named Wabasha." *Collections of the Minnesota Historical Society* 12:503–12. (8)

[208] Wolff, Gerald W. 1975. "Father Sylvester Eisenman and Marty Mission." *South Dakota History* 5:360–89. (24)

[209] Woodruff, K. Brent. 1934. "The Episcopal Mission to the Dakotas, 1860–1898." *South Dakota Historical Collections* 17:553–603. (27)

[210] Woolworth, Alan R. 1974. "Ethnohistorical Report on the Yankton Sioux."

American Indian Ethnohistory Series:
Plains Indians. In *Sioux Indians*, vol. 3.,
pp. 9–245. New York: Garland.   (1)

[211]   Writers' Program, Montana. 1961. *The
Assiniboines: From the Accounts of the Old
Ones Told to First Boy (James Larpenteur
Long)*. Norman: University of Okla-
homa Press.   (29)

[212]*   Writers' Program, South Dakota. 1941.
Legends of the Mighty Sioux. Chicago: A.
Whitman. Reprinted, Sioux Falls, S.D.:
Fantab, 1970.   (35)

[213]   Zimmerman, Bill. 1975. *Airlift to
Wounded Knee*. Chicago: Swallow Press. (18)

The Newberry Library
Center for the History of the American Indian
Founding Director: D'Arcy McNickle
Director: Francis Jennings

Established in 1972 by the Newberry Library, in conjunction with the Committee on Institutional Cooperation of eleven midwestern universities, the Center makes the resources of one of America's foremost research libraries in the Humanities available to those interested in improving the quality and effectiveness of teaching American Indian history. The Newberry's collections include some 100,000 volumes on the history of the American Indian and offer specialized resources for studying historical aspects of Indian-White relations and Indian linguistics. The Center also assists Native Americans engaged in writing tribal histories and developing educational materials.

ADVISORY COMMITTEE

Chairman: Alfonso Ortiz
University of New Mexico

Robert F. Berkhofer
University of Michigan

Robert V. Dumont, Jr.
*Native American Educational Services/Antioch College;
Fort Peck Reservation*

Raymond D. Fogelson
University of Chicago

William T. Hagan
State University of New York College, Fredonia

Nancy O. Lurie
Milwaukee Public Museum

Cheryl Metoyer-Duran
University of California, Los Angeles

N. Scott Momaday
Stanford University

Father Peter J. Powell
St. Augustine Indian Center

Father Paul Prucha, s.j.
Marquette University

Faith Smith
*Native American Educational Services/Antioch College;
Chicago*

Sol Tax
University of Chicago

Robert K. Thomas
Wayne State University

Robert M. Utley
Advisory Council on Historical Preservation; Washington, D.C.

Antoinette McNickle Vogel
Gaithersburg, MD.

Dave Warren
Institute of American Indian Arts

Wilcomb E. Washburn
Smithsonian Institution